DEDICATION

To all the wonderful grandmothers who
have made a difference in their
grandchildren's lives.

And to the greatest grandmother of them
all, my mother,
Maryon (Melé) Mackie.

ACKNOWLEDGMENTS

Thanks to Vera Allen-Smith and Joyce K. Allen
Logan, my two computer wizards and editors
who were indispensable.
Thanks also to my literary agent,
Laurie Harper of Sebastian Agency, who is my
greatest ally, and to Mary Ellen O'Neill and Trish
Todd, my talented editors from Dell Publishing,
who were joys to work with.

GRANDMOTHERS ARE LIKE SNOWFLAKES

...NO TWO ARE ALIKE

JANET LANESE

A Dell Trade Paperback

Grandmothers Are Like Snowflakes

...No Two Are Alike

A Collection

Words of Wisdom, Gentle Advice,
and Hilarious Observations

Janet Lanese

CONTENTS

GRANDMAS THEN AND NOW

It is as grandmothers that our mothers come into the fullness of their grace. When a man's mother holds his child in her gladden arms he is aware of the roundness of life's cycle; of the mystic harmony of life's ways.

Christopher Morley

The birth of a child in the family can be the greatest leveler of differences, bringing everyone together.

Grandma Jan

3

Grandma's home is her grandchildren's second home, a sort of security blanket they can escape to when the world is unfriendly.

Grandma Jan

Parent-child relationships are complex. Grandmother-grandchild relationships are simple. Grandmas are short on criticism and long on love.

Grandma Jan

What's so simple even a small child can
manipulate it?
   Why, a grandmother, of course!

Anonymous

If you would civilize a man, begin with his
grandmother.

Victor Hugo

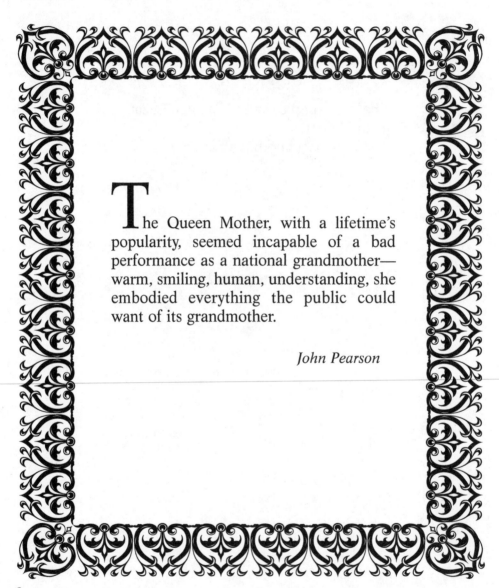

The Queen Mother, with a lifetime's popularity, seemed incapable of a bad performance as a national grandmother—warm, smiling, human, understanding, she embodied everything the public could want of its grandmother.

John Pearson

Since the beginning of time grandmothers have been negotiators and peacemakers in their families.

Grandma Jan

The closest friends I have made all through life have been people who also grew up close to a loved and loving grandmother or grandfather.

Margaret Mead

Children have more need of models than critics.

Joseph Joubert

Children have never been very good at listening to their elders, but they have never failed to imitate them.

James Baldwin

All children wear the sign:

I want to be important NOW!

Many of our juvenile delinquency problems arise because nobody reads the sign.

Dan Pursuit

If a child lives with approval, he learns to live with himself.

 Dorothy Law Nolte

In order not to influence a child, one must be careful not to be that child's parent or grandparent.

Don Marquis

If children grew up according to early indications, we should have nothing but geniuses.

Goethe

Children's children are a crown to the aged,
and parents are the pride of their children.

Proverbs 17:6

Grandchildren restore our zest for life, and
our faith in humanity.

Grandma Jan

ld-fashioned grandmothers take their grandchildren by the hand and lead them into the future. They are safe and kind, and wiser than the child's mother.

Florence King

———————

Our grandchildren accept us for ourselves, without rebuke or effort to change us, as no one in our entire lives has ever done, not our parents, siblings, spouses, friends—and hardly ever our own grown children.

Ruth Goode

The person who has lived the most is not the one with the most years, but the one with the richest experiences.

Jean-Jacques Rousseau

God gave us loving grandchildren as a reward for all our random acts of kindness.

Grandma Jan

There are one hundred and fifty-two
distinctly different ways of holding a baby,
and they are all right.

Heywood Broun

━━━━━━━━━━━━

Whether she is a homemaker
or career woman, all a
grandmother wants is
her family's love and
respect as a
productive individual
who has much to
contribute.

Grandma Jan

Grandchildren don't make a woman feel old; it's being married to a grandfather that bothers her.

Grandma Jan

That flamboyant grandmother wearing black leather and riding a Harley may not fit the picture of an old-fashioned granny, yet she is a confident and free-spirited woman. Her children call her eccentric, but her grandkids call her "cool!"

Grandma Jan

A grandmother is a baby-sitter who watches the kids instead of the television.

Anonymous

Grandchildren are loving reminders of what we're really here for.

Grandma Jan

Grandmothers are voices of the past and role models of the present. Grandmothers open the doors to the future.

Helen Ketchum

My grandmothers are full of memories.

Margaret Walker

===================

My grandma's life was so exciting, it would make a great TV miniseries.

Nathan (age ten)

===================

My great-grandmama told my grandmama the part she lived through that my grandmama didn't live through and my grandmama told my mama what they both lived through and my mama told me what they all lived through and we're supposed to pass it down like that from generation to generation so we'll never forget.

Gayl Jones

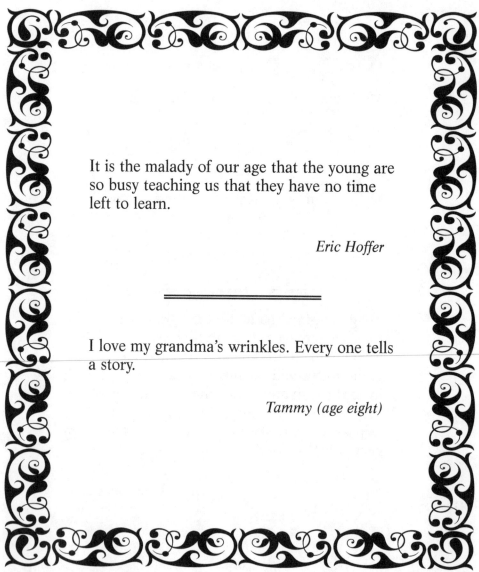

It is the malady of our age that the young are so busy teaching us that they have no time left to learn.

Eric Hoffer

I love my grandma's wrinkles. Every one tells a story.

Tammy (age eight)

◆ ◆ ◆ ◆ ◆ ◆ ◆ ◆ ◆ ◆ ◆ ◆ ◆ ◆ ◆ ◆

Let's bring back grandmothers! A real
family consists of three generations. It's
time Americans stopped worrying about
interference and being a burden on the
children and regrouped under one roof.

Florence King

◆

It's impossible for a grandmother to
understand that few people, and maybe
none, will find her grandchild as endearing
as she does.

Grandma Jan

◆ ◆ ◆ ◆ ◆ ◆ ◆ ◆ ◆ ◆ ◆ ◆ ◆ ◆ ◆ ◆

What families have in common the world around is that they are the place where people learn who they are and how to be that way.

Jean-Illsley Clark

Being a grandmother is our last chance to act like a kid without being accused of being in our second childhood.

Grandma Jan

At Nana's house even my puppy who piddles is welcomed with love.

Dennis (age seven)

When Grandma was a girl, she didn't do things the girls do today. But then the grandmas didn't do the things grandmas do today.

Anonymous

Perfection is in the eyes of those who wear blinders, and nobody wears blinders better than a doting grandmother.

Grandma Jan

The Perks of Grandmotherhood

❤ Your maternal instincts are rekindled

❤ You appreciate the continuity of life

❤ You experience the joy of unconditional love

❤ You start mellowing out

❤ You live every day to its fullest

❤ You're closer to your family

❤ You accept the things you cannot change

❤ You pay attention to your own physical and emotional well-being

❤ You make time for travel and romance

Grandma Jan

 ow! Are grandchildren great!
Spoil them rotten—give them
back—and laugh and laugh.
Revenge is sweet!

Aris Painter

Was there ever a grandparent bushed
after a day of minding noisy youngsters who
hasn't felt the Lord knew what He was
doing when He gave little children to young
people?

Joe E. Wells

MUTUAL ATTRACTION

I could never understand why people were so batty over their grandchildren until mine came into my life. Everything they do, everything they are is precious. I'm looking forward to watching them grow, watching them become.

Sally Stuart

Feeding our grandbabies, burping them, bathing them, changing them, singing to them and cuddling them, are all expressions of our love.

That love is returned to us tenfold before they take their first step.

Grandma Jan

The joys of the grandparent-grandchild bond, the double joys of trust and love.

Grandma Jan

I'm sure my grandmother is reincarnated—she knows too much.

Michael (age thirteen)

Who can resist seeing oneself in miniature?
It is inevitable that your adorable grandbaby
inherits dimples, curly hair, and a button
nose from your side of the family.

Grandma Jan

The only ones who don't notice when your
hair starts graying, your face is sagging, and
your waistline is disappearing are your
grandchildren and the family dog.

Grandma Jan

You know you have been bitten by the grandmother bug when you

♥ See the beauty in a red, wizened newborn's face

♥ Wallpaper the den in Disney characters

♥ Send those ugly hospital baby photos to all your friends and relatives

♥ Pick up your "Grandma's Brag Book" and it's heavier than the family album

♥ Buy the baby a wardrobe whose cost rivals the national debt

♥ Offer to baby-sit on your Bingo night

♥ Start collecting teddy bears

♥ Trade in your sports car for a minivan with a built-in baby seat

♥ Find yourself using baby talk to your husband, until he threatens to "wing your wittle neck"

Grandma Jan

I really don't think of my grandmother as
old, only well seasoned.

Maggie (age fourteen)

A person's maturity consists in having
found again the seriousness one had as a
child at play.

Friedrich Wilhelm Nietzsche

Grandmothers are natural baby-sitters. Who
is more trustworthy or whose fee is more
nominal? For us it is a labor of love.

Grandma Jan

For an old lady, my grandmother's memory is unbelievable. She has eighteen grandchildren and she still remembers all of our names.

Brian (age twelve)

You had no choice about what your given name would be, and you'll probably have about the same chance of influencing your grandchildren about what they will call you. As long as they call you. Grandma, Nana, Mi Mi, and Ounma are all terms of endearment.

Grandma Jan

I love the way my Mi Mi smells. It's sort of a mixture of fresh-baked brownies and that rose perfume old people wear.

Jessica (age ten)

Grandmothers and their grandchildren always seem to be on the same wavelength. Only grandmothers appreciate how wise children are and how much children understand about the world around them.

Grandma Jan

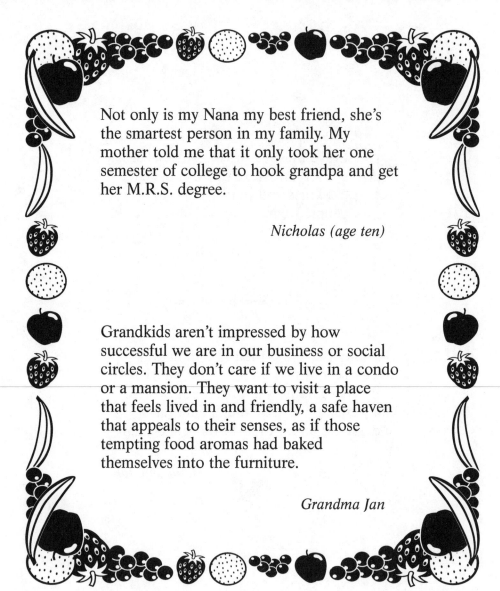

Not only is my Nana my best friend, she's the smartest person in my family. My mother told me that it only took her one semester of college to hook grandpa and get her M.R.S. degree.

Nicholas (age ten)

Grandkids aren't impressed by how successful we are in our business or social circles. They don't care if we live in a condo or a mansion. They want to visit a place that feels lived in and friendly, a safe haven that appeals to their senses, as if those tempting food aromas had baked themselves into the furniture.

Grandma Jan

What Is a Grandmother?
by Patsy Gray (age nine)

A grandmother is a lady who has no children of her own so she likes other people's little girls. A grandfather is a man grandmother. He goes for walks with the boys, and they talk about fishing and tractors, and things like that. Grandmothers don't have to do anything except be there. They're old, so they shouldn't play hard or run. It is enough if they drive us to the market where the pretend horse is and have lots of dimes ready. Or, if they take us for walks, they should slow down past things like pretty leaves and caterpillars. They should never say "Hurry up!"

Usually they are fat, but not too fat to tie a kid's shoes. They wear glasses and funny underwear. They can take their teeth and gums off.

It's better if they don't typewrite or play cards except with us. They don't have to be smart, only answer questions like why dogs hate cats, and how come God isn't married.

They don't talk baby talk like visitors do

because it is hard to understand. When they read to us, they don't skip or mind if it is the same story again.

Everybody should try to have one, especially if you don't have television, because grandmothers are the only grown-ups who have time.

Ruth Goode

My Nana can run the microwave better than any person I know.

Mark (age six)

If grandmas hadn't existed, kids would have inevitably invented them.

Arthur Kornhaber, M.D.

Though the world has changed around us, grandmothers and grandchildren still share an emotional bond that is one of life's most powerful experiences.

Grandma Jan

My grandma is so great, she's almost worth her weight in chocolate fudge brownies.

Jeffrey (age eleven)

Children love to laugh, to be around grown-ups who can laugh at themselves and at life. Grandmothers have learned the more laughter they have in their lives, the better. That's why grandmothers keep children's spirits soaring.

Grandma Jan

 My grandma and Santa Claus are my very favorite people. I think they're about the same age.

Jessica (age five)

Some of my best friends are children. In fact, all of my best friends are children.

J. D. Salinger

My grandma is the funnest person I know. She goes to all my ball games, plays Monopoly with me, and takes me to Disneyland.

Marcy (age six)

Grandmothers rarely get disheartened about their grandchildren's mistakes. Grandmothers regard their grandchildren's blunders merely as stepping-stones to success.

Grandma Jan

All elders should have at least one youngster to be "crazy about" and vice versa. Grandparenting supplies the role model for a healthy and fulfilling old age. And grandchildren want grandparents.

Arthur Kornhaber, M.D.

I love my grandma because no matter how many stupid things I do, she still tells all her friends that I am the smartest boy alive.

Mark (age seven)

Your sons weren't made to like you. That's
what grandchildren are for.

Jane Smiley

Every child comes with the message that
God is not yet discouraged of man.

Rabindranath Tagore

Why are grandmothers nicer than mothers?
Because they don't believe in spanking,
that's why!

Melanie (age six)

THAT MAGIC TOUCH

When it seems the world can't understand,
Your grandmother's there to hold your
hand.

With her gentle words and open heart
Your grandmother shares with graceful art.

Her adoring eyes see just the best
Your grandmother will ignore the rest.

A grandmother's love means oh, so much!
Your grandmother has that magic touch.

Joyce K. Allen Logan

It is our right as grandmothers to love
unconditionally.

Grandma Jan

Grandchildren have the magic of putting
the fun back into middle age.

Grandma Jan

How wonderful to have Grandma to
complain to when I'm mad at my parents.

Carolyn (age ten)

Every grandmother enriches her
grandchildren's lives in her own special way.

Grandma Jan

Like the sun, a grandmother's love shines
on her grandchildren, nourishing their
emotional and spiritual growth.

Grandma Jan

No other family member can encourage,
support, and boost a child's self-esteem like
a grandmother.

Grandma Jan

A truly appreciative child will break, lose,
spoil or fondle to death any really successful
gift within a matter of minutes.

Russell Lynes

Nothing offends children more than to play
down to them. All the greatest children's
books—*The Pilgrim's Progress, Robinson
Crusoe, Grimm's Fairy Tales* and *Gulliver's
Travels*—were written for adults.

George Bernard Shaw

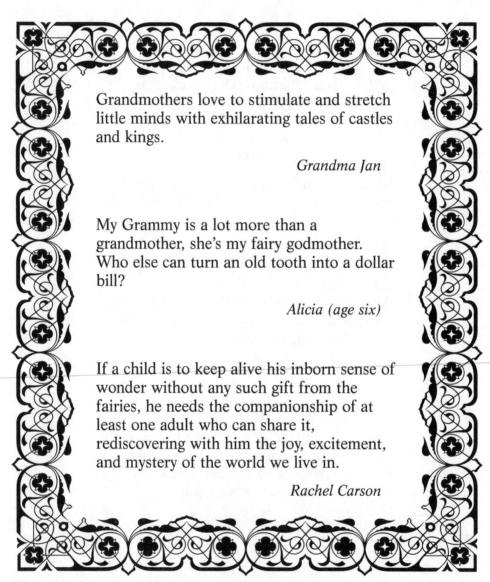

Grandmothers love to stimulate and stretch little minds with exhilarating tales of castles and kings.

Grandma Jan

My Grammy is a lot more than a grandmother, she's my fairy godmother. Who else can turn an old tooth into a dollar bill?

Alicia (age six)

If a child is to keep alive his inborn sense of wonder without any such gift from the fairies, he needs the companionship of at least one adult who can share it, rediscovering with him the joy, excitement, and mystery of the world we live in.

Rachel Carson

No one has yet fully realized the wealth of sympathy, kindness, and generosity hidden in the soul of a child. The effort of every true education should be to unlock that treasure.

Emma Goldman

Nothing brings greater joy to grandchildren and grandmothers than entering together into a world of fantasy and wonder.

Grandma Jan

There is still a child in all of us who has always believed in miracles. To children miracles are simple things. Every day is miraculous—unexplained, inspiring, ever new.

Karen Goldman

Children know the grace of God better than most of us. They see the world the way the morning brings it back to them. New and born and fresh and wonderful.

Archibald MacLeish

A grandmother's love is a powerful potion.

Grandma Jan

A Grandma's Lullaby

Little one, precious one,
    Time to go off to sleep now.

Hush-a-bye, don't you cry,
    Time to go off to Dreamland.

Morning will come and your sunshine smile
    Lights our hearts so sweetly.

Little one, precious one,
    Grandma loves you forever.

Ann M. Sherman-Simpson

What children expect from grandparents is
not to be understood but to be loved.

Grandma Jan

So many things we love are you!

I can't seem to explain except
by little things, but flowers and
beautiful handmade things—Small stitches

So much of reading and thinking—
so many sweet customs and so much of
our . . . well, our religion. It is all you.

I hadn't realized it before. This is so
vague but do you see a little, dear
Grandma? I want to thank you.

from "Bring Me a Unicorn"
by Anne Morrow Lindbergh

A grandmother magically uses her grandchildren's eyes and hearts to see and feel as they do. She tries to see things from their point of view.

Grandma Jan

Grandmothers love questions like

❤ Which cows give chocolate milk?

❤ Is there really a man in the moon?

❤ How do birds fly?

❤ Does the Easter bunny lay eggs?

❤ If the earth is round, why don't we fall off?

❤ Do flowers sleep at night?

Grandma Jan

A grandmother's patience is a like a tube of toothpaste—never quite all gone.

Grandma Jan

A grandmother is an overly fussy person who spits on her handkerchief and wipes imaginary smudges off your face.

Kimberly (age eight)

Family faces are magic mirrors. Looking at people who belong to us, we see the past, present, and future.

Gail Lumet Buckley

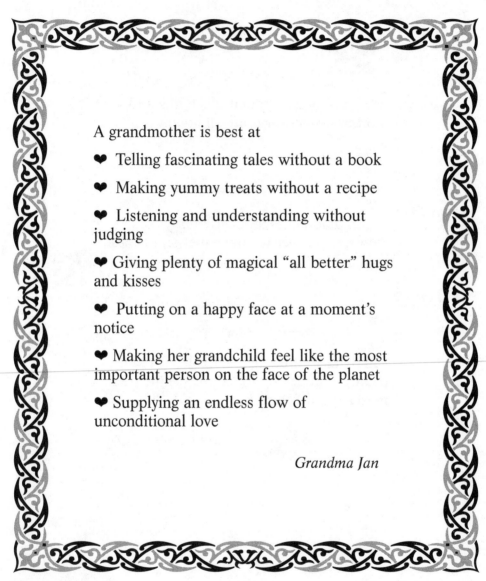

A grandmother is best at

- ❤ Telling fascinating tales without a book

- ❤ Making yummy treats without a recipe

- ❤ Listening and understanding without judging

- ❤ Giving plenty of magical "all better" hugs and kisses

- ❤ Putting on a happy face at a moment's notice

- ❤ Making her grandchild feel like the most important person on the face of the planet

- ❤ Supplying an endless flow of unconditional love

Grandma Jan

If nothing is going well, call your grandmother or grandfather.

Italian proverb

Hugs and kisses are even grander when they are given by a loving grandmother.

Grandma Jan

Once you've loved a child, you will love all children. You give away your love to one, and you find that by giving you've made yourself an inexhaustible treasury.

Margaret Lee Runbeck

The secret that makes grandma's cooking taste so terrific is that she always adds a spoonful of love.

Grandma Jan

Grandmothers are like Kleenex: soft, strong and able to absorb the hurts of a small child.

Grandma Jan

Grandma was kind of a first-aid station, or a Red Cross nurse, who took up where the battle ended, accepting us and our little sobbing sins, gathering the whole of us into her lap, restoring us to health and confidence by her amazing faith in life, and in a mortal's strength to use it.

Lillian Smith

My Nana is the only person in the whole world that I let hold my tongue down with a stick, give me nasty-tasting medicine, and put a thermometer in a place I shouldn't mention.

Jason (age six)

Grandmothers of every race and country have a legendary role as healers: Jewish grandmothers make chicken soup, others have their own special remedies. When a child in a North American Yurok Indian tribe is ill, Grandmother goes out into the wilderness to intervene with the spirits by singing and speaking to them. Every grandmother has her own song.

Arthur Kornhaber, M.D.

Out of love, parents teach their children to be wary of new things. Out of love, grandmothers encourage their grandchildren to take a chance and conquer the unknown.

Grandma Jan

Grandma begs my parents to go out for the evening so she can be alone with me.

Sarah (age four)

A grandchild represents a world in us, a world nonexistent before his birth. Once a grandmother, a woman is reborn into a new world, one filled with hope and expectations.

Grandma Jan

Grandmothering comes not from the head but from the heart.

Grandma Jan

OUR LITTLE ANGELS

 A baby is God's opinion that the world should go on.

Carl Sandburg

A newborn baby . . . is without question the most phenomenal, the most astonishing, the most absolutely unparalleled thing that has yet occurred in the entire history of this planet.

Irvin S. Cobb

Babies are such a nice way to start people.

Don Herold

Something to live for came to place
   Something to die for maybe

Something to give even sorrow a grace
   And yet it was only a baby

Harriet Spofford

Every baby born into the world is a finer
one than the last.

Charles Dickens

The secret of a happy life is to skip having
children and go directly to the
grandchildren.

Momma
(cartoon character created by Mel Lazarus)

It is the rare grandmother who doesn't think her grandchild is constantly growing toward the pinnacle of perfection.

Grandma Jan

The first grandchild is a thrill, but the second and third ones are just as delightful. Each one is a fresh, unique personality, a tiny but distinct human being whom you've never known before.

Grandma Jan

Rapture and euphoria are weak attempts at describing the bliss I felt watching the birth of my granddaughter.

Vera Allen-Smith

Children are like puppies; you have to keep them near you and look after them if you want their affection.

Anna Magnani

Children divine those who love them; it is a gift of nature which we lose as we grow up.

Paul de Kock

Even if the first third of your life was dominated by your parents, and the second third by your children, you still have your grandchildren to salvage the remainder.

Grandma Jan

Not all of us think grandkids are the greatest—but that was before I met mine.

Jane Russell

My three grandchildren, Christopher, Melanie, and Matthew, are the perfect age—too old for strollers and too young to borrow my car.

Grandma Jan

The kind sweet souls who love, cherish, inspire and protect their grandchildren are not guardian angels; they are grandmothers.

Bettye "Mi Mi" Flynn

This tiny new granddaughter
Is a thing of wonder
Of beauty.
How perfect her fingers,
Her feathery eyelashes,
Her sweet mouth.

My heart is full to overflowing
As I hold her in my arms,
Touch her cheek with one finger,
Know she will always be—
My granddaughter.

C. S. Thoni

A new grandson
Our family line moves on
How beautiful this day
How wonderful this child
With such shining eyes
And smooth skin.

A new grandson
Brings joy and hope
For a brighter, happier future.

C. S. Thoni

Children are likely to live up to what
you believe of them.

Lady Bird Johnson

Dearer than our children are the children of
our children.

Egyptian proverb

 Grandchildren are magical creatures
you can lock out of your kitchen, but
never out of your heart.

Grandma Jan

This grandchild, so new and small,
   with tiny hands and large bright eyes
Brings life to the world, a fresh beginning
   filled with endless surprises and new
   discoveries.

The fullness of life shines in this tiny face,
   familiar features: nose and chin, a
   dimpled cheek
Bring love and joy to life. A family grows
   toward a future of possibility and
   promise.

Joyce K. Allen Logan

Perfect love sometimes does not come until the first grandchild.

Welsh proverb

I'm not a picture-toting grandma—but my grandchildren just happen to be the best-looking children in the continental United States, and you can throw in Canada and the Virgin Islands.

Abigail Van Buren

A grandmother proudly wheeled her grandchild into the park. An acquaintance came by, peeked into the carriage and said, "My, what a gorgeous child!"

The grandmother said, "Wait until you see her pictures!"

Milton Berle

My grandkids' visits are special times, filled
with lots of hugs and kisses, sighs and cries.
I enjoy these times, but it's still a relief to
know their parents will take over again at
the end of the day.

Barbara Wallis

By the time the youngest children have
learned to keep the place tidy, the oldest
grandchildren are on hand to tear it to
pieces.

Christopher Morley

What feeling is so nice as a child's hand in
yours? So small, so soft and warm, like a
kitten huddling in the shelter of your clasp.

Marjorie Holmes

How to Eat Like a Child

Spinach:
1. Divide into little piles. Rearrange again into new piles.

2. After five or six maneuvers, sit back and say you are full.

Ice-cream cone:
1. Ask for a double scoop. Knock the top scoop off while walking out the door of the ice-cream parlor. Cry.

2. Lick the remaining scoop slowly so that the ice cream melts down the outside of the cone and over your hand. Stop licking when the ice cream is even with the top of the cone. Be sure it is absolutely even.

3. Eat a hole in the bottom of the cone and suck the rest of the ice cream out of the bottom.

4. When only the cone remains with ice cream coating the inside, leave on car dashboard.

Chocolate-chip cookies:

1. Half-sit, half-lie on the bed, propped up by a pillow. Read a book. Place cookies next to you on the sheet so that the crumbs get in the bed.

2. As you eat the cookies, remove each chocolate chip and place it on your stomach.

3. When all the cookies are consumed, eat the chips one by one, allowing two per page.

Delia Ephron

My Granddaughter Is . . .

A bell of laughter shattering
   the morning sun

A crystal gift of tears for me
   to wipe away

A present joy that now is more
   than I can ever say

A promise of a future when
   my days are done

Dorcas Moyer

Children in a family are like
flowers in a bouquet. There's
always one determined to face in an
opposite direction from the way
the arranger desires.

Madeline Cox

71

A grandma is a bossy lady who orders you
to put on a sweater when she's chilly and to
go to bed when she's tired—tired of you,
that is.

Mark (age nine)

The persons hardest to convince they're at
retirement age are children at bedtime.

Shanon Fife

Children ask better questions than do
adults. "May I have a cookie?" "Why is the
sky blue?" and "What does a cow say?" are
far more likely to elicit a cheerful response
than "Where's your manuscript?" and
"Who's your lawyer?"

Fran Lebowitz

As long as her grandchild is having fun playing games, a grandmother doesn't place a lot of emphasis on winning. But don't let another adult criticize the little tyke! It's no wonder grandmas and Little League umpires don't get along.

Grandma Jan

Heirlooms we don't have in our family. But stories we've got.

Kim Chernin

My grandma tells me she keeps the family skeletons in the closet, but I've looked and looked and I still can't find them.

Sarah (age five)

You know children are growing up when they start asking questions that have answers.

John J. Plomp

Just how ambitious was Grandma Jones when it came to her grandchildren? Well, when a stranger inquired as to their ages, she replied, "The doctor's in the third grade and the rocket scientist is in the fifth."

Anonymous

My grandma looks exactly like my mom, only more lumpy.

Jonathan (age eight)

Grandchildren are a renewal of life, a little bit of us going on into the future.

Helene Schellenberg Barnhart

Grandmothers are older than they look. I heard many of them go back to World War II.

Susan (age nine)

What Is a Grandson?

A grandson is that other man in Grandmother's life who has her wrapped right around his finger. A bewitching creature sprinkled with stardust, a grandson is heaven-sent, and only one step below perfection. A grandson is purity in dirty sneakers, chivalry on a carousel horse, and beauty with a milk mustache. No matter how small his size, a grandson is big in spirit.

A grandson is a player of nonsensical computer games, a dreamer of flights to other galaxies, and an avid collector of useless trinkets. A quick study in perpetual motion, a grandson pauses long enough to gulp down a snack, glance at the TV, flip through a comic book, or eavesdrop on Grandmother's telephone conversation.

A grandson is a gentle prankster with an impish grin and a jolly laugh whose spontaneous wit keeps Grandmother on her toes. Though he dismisses Grandmother's bear hugs and wet kisses as "baby stuff," a grandson never fails to tell her that she is the best grandma in the world. A grandson is the captor who holds the key to Grandmother's heart.

Grandma Jan

What Is a Granddaughter?

A granddaughter is the most exciting thing that can happen to an empty-nester. A charismatic angel with slightly frayed wings, she fills Grandmother's home with energetic activity and contagious laughter. Where there is love, there is usually a granddaughter near by.

A granddaughter is grace on Rollerblades, independence parading around in father's best shirt, and brilliance building sand castles. A granddaughter is Grandmother's closest confidante and best friend. Enchanting, amusing, inquisitive, and wise beyond her years, a granddaughter has the power to renew Grandmother's spirit and expand her universe in a twinkle of an eye.

A granddaughter is a pint-sized bolt of lightning who relishes turning Grandmother's daily routine topsy-turvy. If a granddaughter is not bombarding Grandmother with hypothetical questions or begging her to play ball, she's into the cookie jar. But when she finally winds down, climbs up on Grandmother's lap, and whispers those magical words "Hold me, Grandma," a granddaughter is pure bliss.

Grandma Jan

Reflection

Tonight my small grandson
Consults the mirror.
With five-year-old aplomb
He condenses the universe
Into that shining square.

One light winks out.
A shadow falls across his face.
His fingers touch one cheek, still bright.
"This is morning," he says,
"And this is night."

The enormity of earth is tailored
To fit in his reflection.
His glance compresses ages, solves mysteries.
I find in his features, briefly seen there
The same answer he finds in the mirror.

Dorcas Moyer

A grandchild should never be loved for love returned; a grandchild should be loved for himself, and nothing else.

Grandma Jan

A grandmother is a woman who's thrilled because her grandchild can recite the Gettysburg Address at eight when Lincoln didn't do it until he was much older.

Milton Berle

Children are remarkable for their
intelligence and ardor, for their curiosity,
their intolerance of shams, the clarity and
ruthlessness of their vision.

Aldous Huxley

Pretty much all the honest truth telling
there is in the world is done by children.

Oscar Wilde

GENERATIONS
OF LOVE

When you look at your life, the greatest happinesses are family happinesses.

Dr. Joyce Brothers

Nobody can share a lifetime of experience and family legacies with a child the way a grandmother can.

Grandma Jan

Whatever their backgrounds or interests, grandmothers share common ground. They enjoy special family recipes or dishes, they share family jokes, common expressions or songs, and they participate in traditions and special events that bring the family together.

But most important of all, they're crazy about their grandchildren, and will go to the ends of the earth to play multiple roles as nurturers, caregivers, mentors, and wizards to them.

Grandma Jan

Over the river and through the wood.
  Now grandmother's cap I spy!

Hurray for the fun!
  Is the pudding done?
  Hurrah for the pumpkin pie!

Lydia Maria Child

Even a minor event in the life of a child is
an event of that child's world, and thus a
world event.

Gaston Bachelard

Listening children know stories are there.
When their elders sit and begin, children
are just waiting and hoping for one to come
out, like a mouse from a hole.

Eudora Welty

Some grandmas love to cook
Others prefer a good book

Some grandmas go to work each day
Others are retired and choose to play

Some grandmas are jolly and funny
Others are classy, loaded with money

Every grandma has a different face
All cherished in their special place

Deep in their grandchildren's hearts

Grandma Jan

My mother, now a great-grandmother, still
keeps all the children mesmerized with tales
of her escapades as a silent-screen extra.
With exciting stories of mobsters and the
stock market crash and vivid descriptions of
the clothing, entertainment, and headlines
of the time, she has recaptured a golden era
for three generations of family members.

Grandma Jan

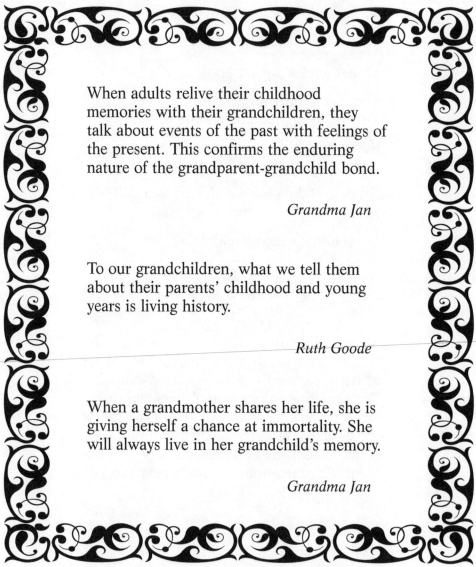

When adults relive their childhood memories with their grandchildren, they talk about events of the past with feelings of the present. This confirms the enduring nature of the grandparent-grandchild bond.

Grandma Jan

To our grandchildren, what we tell them about their parents' childhood and young years is living history.

Ruth Goode

When a grandmother shares her life, she is giving herself a chance at immortality. She will always live in her grandchild's memory.

Grandma Jan

My grandmother remembers with her heart
those tender little childhood moments that I
have long forgotten.

Joyce K. Allen Logan

From a Grateful Granddaughter

For as long as I can remember you were
always there
To teach me how to love others,
and how to love myself . . .
And to look for the good in everyone.
You were always there to listen,
to hold my hand, and to hug me.

Your joy for life and nurturing care
Have been a major influence in my life.

Thank you for being my grandmother.

Frieda McReynolds

Grandparents impart history and values by
their very existence; it made the existence of
their grandchildren possible.

Robert A. Aldrich, M.D.
and Glenn Austin, M.D.

Posterity is the patriotic name for
grandchildren.

Art Linkletter

It is always self-defeating to pretend to the
style of a generation younger than your
own; it simply erases your own experience
in history.

Renata Adler

The moment a baby is born, a grandmother
is born too.

Grandma Jan

The birth of a grandchild is like the arrival of Spring, awakening from a deep Winter's sleep and budding forth with new life, bringing joy and optimism for the future.

Vera Allen-Smith

. . . I'm going to ask something of every one of you.

Let me start with my generation—the grandparents out there.

You are our living link to the past. Tell your grandchildren the story of the struggles waged, at home and abroad. Of sacrifices freely made for freedom's sake. And tell them your own story as well—because every American has a story to tell.

George Bush

Children are a great comfort in your old age—and they help you reach it faster too.

Lionel Kaufman

My Nana is awesome! She is the only one in my family who can boss my mom around and get away with it.

Jeffrey (age nine)

Any activity we enjoy with our grandchildren can become a family tradition: walks on the beach, playing charades, visiting a favorite ice-cream parlor, decorating Easter eggs, and even picking out a new pair of school shoes. These are events memories are made of, simple rituals which are passed from generation to generation.

Grandma Jan

As the years go by and my grandchildren grow older, I will no longer be in demand to baby-sit, read fairy tales, or ride the merry-go-round. How I dread that day! But if I'm lucky, there will be another time, another place, and other children. For someday I'll be a great-grandmother.

Grandma Jan

Nothing has the power to make you believe in miracles again like a new grandbaby.

Grandma Jan

A new grandbaby is about the size of a hug.

Grandma Jan

Loving Legacy

1. Begin showing small children photographs of themselves as babies and photos of other family members. Point out family resemblances and tell brief stories about the different pictures to help children develop a sense of belonging.

2. Tell stories from your childhood that have counterparts with situations in your grandchildren's lives.

3. Keep a journal, a kind of life-book. Even if children are not interested in hearing your stories and other family history now, they may be later.

4. Capture your grandchild's interest and imagination by bringing out memorabilia, such as yearbooks, records, souvenirs, clothing, and posters.

5. Consider making an audio or video tape of your life story or vignettes from your family's history.

6. Old folk songs and nursery rhymes are a wonderful way to communicate with youngsters. Sing them songs your mother taught you, the same ones they will teach their children.

Grandma Jan

You'll never forget when and where you first heard the news you had become a grandmother. All the joy wrapped up in that tiny bundle of love sparks a renewal in your relationship with your family that will be enhanced as the baby grows.

Grandma Jan

I suddenly realized that through no act of my own I had become biologically related to a new human being.

Margaret Mead

The joy of becoming a mother was a prelude to the elation of becoming a grandmother.

Vera Allen-Smith

Mrs. Margaret Thatcher informed the world with regal panache yesterday that her daughter-in-law had given birth to a son.

"We have become a grandmother," the Prime Minister said.

as quoted in the London Times, *March 4, 1989*

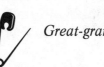

It was a thrill becoming a mother and a joy becoming a grandmother, but nothing can come close to the delight of becoming a great-grandmother.

> *Great-grandma Melé*
> *Mother of Grandma Jan*
> *Grandmother of Lance*
> *Great-grandmother of Christopher,*
> *Melanie, and Matthew*

There is nothing more complimentary than wheeling your three-month-old grandson down the avenue and having a passerby ask if you're his mother.

> *Grandma Jan*

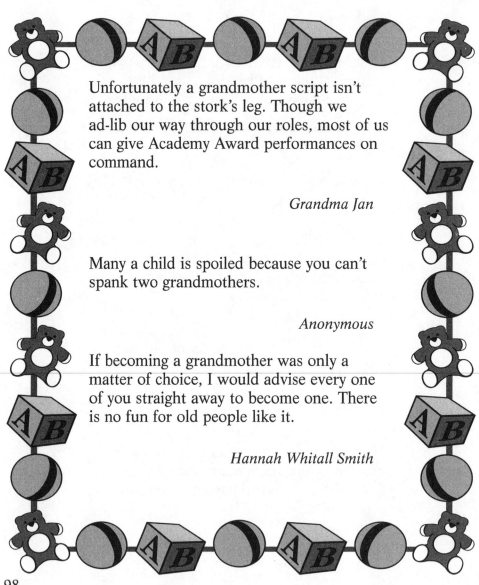

Unfortunately a grandmother script isn't attached to the stork's leg. Though we ad-lib our way through our roles, most of us can give Academy Award performances on command.

Grandma Jan

Many a child is spoiled because you can't spank two grandmothers.

Anonymous

If becoming a grandmother was only a matter of choice, I would advise every one of you straight away to become one. There is no fun for old people like it.

Hannah Whitall Smith

Once your children are grown up and have children of their own, the problems are theirs, and the less the older generation interferes the better.

Eleanor Roosevelt

No cowgirl was ever faster on the draw than a grandma pulling baby pictures out of her handbag.

Anonymous

You often meet grandparents who bore you about their grandchildren, but never vice versa.

Anonymous

You know a grandmother is a goner on her grandchild when she

❤ Nurses every sniffle as if were life-threatening

❤ Looks upon every crayon scrawl as creative genius

❤ Never misses a Little League game, recital, or spelling bee

❤ Insists she recognizes the potential of a "born leader"

❤ Makes up portfolios for talent agencies

❤ Frames all outstanding report cards

❤ Takes more family videos than the Kennedys

❤ Only goes to movies that are rated G

❤ Swears that *Goodnight Moon* is her favorite book

Grandma Jan

God gives us grandchildren so that we can undo some of the mistakes we made as parents.

Grandma Jan

———————————

Grandmother: "Did I tell you about my grandchildren?"

Friend: "No, and I appreciate it very much."

Milton Berle

———————————

Just about the time a woman thinks she can relax and take it easy, she becomes a grandmother.

Grandma Jan

A grandmother suspects she's entering her "golden years" when her husband orders a martini with a prune.

Anonymous

The largest segment of today's grandmothers is too young to take up croquet and too old to rush the net.

Grandma Jan

The three stages of grandmotherhood—youthful, mature, and "you're looking wonderful!"

Grandma Jan

T o a grandmother of a ten-year-old linebacker, any football game he plays in becomes a nervous breakdown divided into quarters.

Grandma Jan

My favorite sweatshirt was a gift from my daughter-in-law Marie. In big, bold letters it announces that I am a

**PROUD MEMBER
OF THE
GRANDMA CLUB**

Grandma Jan

Even if you have resisted the idea of becoming a grandmother, you'll soon find it is one of life's greatest joys. Gazing into that sweet innocent face, grasping those tiny, soft hands, rocking a tiny bundle of joy who is a loving extension of you; what a midlife ecstasy!

Grandma Jan

GRANDMA JAN SAYS

It's a wise grandmother who understands
her strengths and weaknesses and helps her
grandchildren to understand their own.

Grandma Jan

Grandchildren come into our lives, bask in
our love, and return it to us in their special
ways. Yet we cannot live through them.
Like our children they are not ours to own;
they belong to the world. We must give our
grandchildren wings and teach them to fly.

Grandma Jan

The best way a grandmother can get her
grandchildren to listen to her is to listen to
them.

Grandma Jan

A grandma can expand her grandchild's view of the universe.

Grandma Jan

The most valued grandmother asks her children and grandchildren "What can I do for you?" and then does it.

Grandma Jan

A loving grandmother doesn't compare her grandchildren to others. She values each of them for their own special gifts.

Grandma Jan

The greatest gift you can give your grandchild is yourself.

Grandma Jan

Grandmothering holds the greatest rewards for those who put their best efforts into it.

Grandma Jan

Already people over sixty-five outnumber teenagers. As their numbers increase, grandmothers will be powerful spokeswomen in the twenty-first century. Our children and grandchildren look to us for leadership. Being the best we can provides them with positive role models.

Grandma Jan

Grandparenting is an education. Grandparents and grandchildren learn from one another.

Grandma Jan

One grandmother is worth a hundred educators.

Grandma Jan

A grandma doesn't need a Ph.D. in Child Development to be a great teacher. Her grandchildren learn by emulating the person they admire the most.

Grandma Jan

arents are those who learn from their parents.

Grandma Jan

Most grandmothers are proud of the way their children are rearing their grandchildren in today's difficult society. Unfortunately their words of approval are rarely voiced. A little praise goes a long way toward a closer bond and a deeper trust between grandparents and parents.

Grandma Jan

There should never be a power struggle between parents and grandparents, only open communication and a spirit of cooperation.

Grandma Jan

A grandmother's idea of what makes a good parent may have no validity to a young couple with a different belief system.

Grandma Jan

A wise grandmother has no opinions at all when it comes to raising her grandkids. She lets the parents do it their way.

Grandma Jan

You'll hit the top of the parent popularity parade if you give your adult children

1. Respect

2. Acceptance

3. Understanding

4. Support

5. Love

6. Advice (only when asked)

7. Encouragement

8. Appreciation

9. Help

10. Praise

Grandma Jan

You'll plummet to the bottom of the
popularity list if you show them

1. Irreverence

2. Superiority

3. Contention

4. Opposition

5. Scorn

6. Interference

7. Judgment

8. Belittlement

9. Indifference

10. Criticism

Grandma Jan

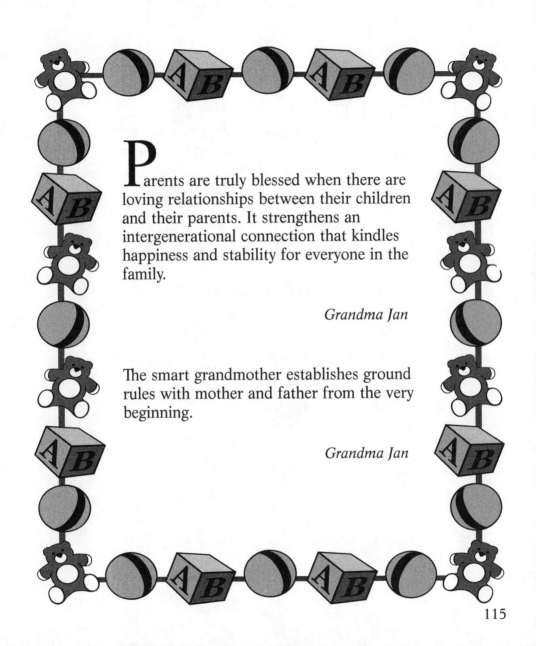

Parents are truly blessed when there are loving relationships between their children and their parents. It strengthens an intergenerational connection that kindles happiness and stability for everyone in the family.

Grandma Jan

The smart grandmother establishes ground rules with mother and father from the very beginning.

Grandma Jan

The best way for a grandmother to stay young is to live honestly, work industriously, exercise regularly, eat sensibly, sleep sufficiently, and avoid telling her age.

Grandma Jan

You don't need to be a super grandma for your grandkids to cherish you. One treasured memory can last a lifetime.

Grandma Jan

Long-distance grandparenting is possible!
The miles can be bridged with phone calls,
photos, letters, tapes, videos, and a monthly
supply of homemade goodies.

Grandma Jan

Lap time with your grandchild is quality
time.

Grandma Jan

More Grandmothers

Are Like Snowflakes

. . . No Two Are Alike

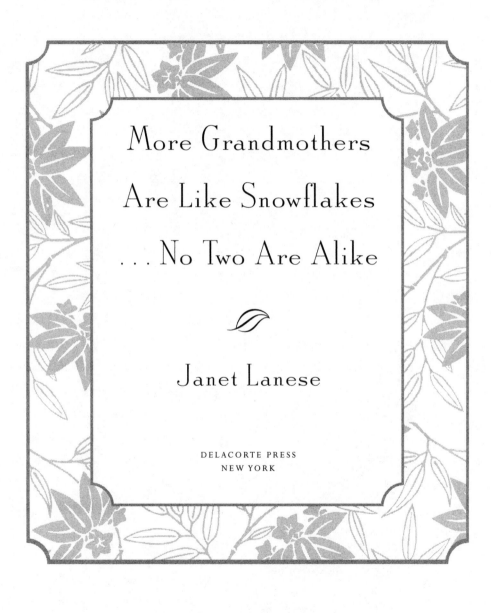

More Grandmothers
Are Like Snowflakes
. . . No Two Are Alike

Janet Lanese

DELACORTE PRESS
NEW YORK

To my wonderful friend Bettye "MiMi" Flynn

and all the terrific grandmothers

of the new millennium who, in a fast-track society,

never waver from their old-fashioned values.

Acknowledgments

Thanks to Super Editor Danielle Perez, whose patience and guidance kept me grounded, and to her assistant Shannon Jamieson for her invaluable help. Also, thanks to Super Agent Laurie Harper, who is always my inspiration.

Contents

Forever Spring

You're never too old to become younger.

Mae West

One positive advantage to age for me is that I have more time to smell the roses.

Helen Hayes

Youth is transitory, but a youthful spirit need never grow old.

Dr. Criswell Freeman

Love is the great beautifier.

Louisa May Alcott

My niece, the weary mother of six, was asked one Sunday morning by the parish priest, "Well, Sue, what do you want your next one to be?"

"A grandchild," she snapped!

Grandma Jan

There is a fountain of youth. It is your mind, your talents, the creativity you bring to your life and the lives of people you love. When you learn to tap this source, you will truly have defeated age.

Sophia Loren

Does becoming a grandma
Leave you aghast?
I'm sorry to say
Life goes by that fast.

Mary McBride

Though it sounds absurd, it is true to say I felt younger at sixty than I felt at twenty.

Ellen Glasgow

Isn't it terrific that you don't have to look like a grandmother to be one?

Grandma Jan

Whether you become a grandma in your mid-twenties or in your senior-citizen-discount years, it's unlikely you'll fit the stereotypical pink-faced, snowy-haired, cookie-baking, chubby old lady. Well, not until you've lived a few more decades at least.

Patricia "Poppy" Smith

I was grossed out when I heard Grandma had a boyfriend at her age! With me and Dad, you'd think two men in her life would be all she could handle.

Donald, age 12

One should never trust a woman who tells her real age. A woman who would tell that would tell anything.

Oscar Wilde

The New-Millennium Grandmother
has switched from—

- ✾ polyester to denim
- ✾ bifocals to contacts
- ✾ cold cream to Retin-A
- ✾ sherry to merlot
- ✾ sedans to SUVs
- ✾ mobile homes to condos
- ✾ curlers to blow dryers
- ✾ manicures to silk or acrylics
- ✾ knitting to exercising
- ✾ banana splits to low-fat yogurt
- ✾ Niagara Falls to Las Vegas
- ✾ J.C. Penney to QVC
- ✾ Paul Newman to Mel Gibson
- ✾ homemaker to entrepreneur
- ✾ snail-mail to e-mail

Grandma Jan

When the grandmothers of today hear the word "Chippendales," they don't necessarily think of chairs.

Jean Kerr

What's an aging boomer to do? You can laser away your wrinkles, tuck your tummy, and make yourself look 25 again; but no matter what you do, there's still one thing that's going to remind you—and everyone else—that you're getting old.

It's that cute little kid following you around in the supermarket shouting, "Grandma, buy me some ice cream!"

Armin Brott

Sometimes it's almost impossible for a grandmother not to look more glamorous than her daughter and daughter-in-law. Especially when the young mother's everyday attire is a stained T-shirt and faded blue jeans. We have much less responsibility, and more time and resources to look like a model from the cover of *Modern Maturity*. So when you go to visit your grandbaby, leave the cosmetics, jewelry, and the designer frocks at home. Have you ever tried to get sour formula out of a silk dress?

Grandma Jan

A good feeling inside is worth more than a great beautician.

Mother Teresa

In youth we learn. In age we understand.

Marie Abner-Eschenbach

NEIGHBOR TO LITTLE GIRL: "How old is your grandmother?"
LITTLE GIRL: "I'm not sure, but I think she's in the middle ages."

Grandma Jan

My grandma refuses to divulge her age. She keeps telling me she's as old as her nose, and a little older than her teeth.

Susan, age 13

Having the ability to love makes a big difference in staying young.

Dinah Shore

A birthday is the one time that a grandmother wants her past forgotten and her present remembered.

Grandma Jan

When my grandma gets all dressed up in a short skirt and high heels, she outclasses my mom. She has better legs.

Samantha, age 16

Real grandmothers don't retire, and they don't fade away; they just get better.

Therese McGee

The most challenging age for a grandmother is poundage.

Grandma Jan

Last summer, I had a great time backpacking with Grandma around Europe. I couldn't believe it, but I had a hard time keeping up with her.

Lonnie, age 17

Age is something that doesn't matter, unless you are a cheese.

Billie Burke

My parents are kinda nerdy, but my grandma looks real cool in her red BMW convertible.

Michael, age 10

Becoming a grandmother is wonderful. One moment you're just a mother. The next you are all-wise and prehistoric.

Pam Brown

So many of us are at that awkward age—too young for Medicare and too old for men to care.

Grandma Jan

Not me? I was dumbfounded, speechless, and a little perturbed to say the least. I'm thirty-six years old. I AM NOT OLD ENOUGH TO BE A GRANDMOTHER!

Well, time has passed and I now have 16 of the little darlin's running around. The funny thing is I wouldn't trade one of them for all the gold in the Klondike. Yes, as the years passed, the wrinkles came and stayed. The gray hair shot out of my grandmotherly head, and the aches and pains have become more real every year.

I have spent a lot of time and money seeking out the perfect moisturizers, hair dyes, and miracle cures in my battle against aging. If there's a vitamin, herb, or chemical that aids in retarding the aging process, I have it, or will soon find it. I will not go quietly into that good night. I love being a mother, and grandmother, but I will always be a woman. Why should my determination to look my best diminish just because my children got older?

Speaking of which, I now am advising them to start young before the day comes when they look in the mirror and shriek: "I am too young to be a grandmother!"

Candalee Swayze

At a time in life when many women are starting to slow down, some grandmothers are just getting started, inspired, perhaps, by the sound of young voices calling out their names, by the sight of finger paintings held to refrigerators by magnets, or by the feel of a tiny hand held under a much larger one.

Mary Grace Rodarte

So what if my grandma has wrinkles? To me they're just happy lines of love.

Stephanie, age 9

You know you're getting old when your grandchild asks you to close your eyes so she can give you a surprise, and you don't wake up until the following afternoon.

Martha Bolton

Something magical happens when parents turn into grandparents. Their attitude changes from "money doesn't grow on trees" to spending it like it does.

Paula Linden

Things from our childhood that our grandkids will never see—

- Howdy Doody puppets
- peashooters
- Powerhouse candy bars
- candy lipstick
- tableside jukeboxes in coffee shops
- home milk delivery in glass bottles
- movies preceded by cartoons and newsreels
- rotary phones and party lines
- drive-ins with carhops
- P. F. Flyers
- sock hops
- bouffant hairdos
- flattop haircuts
- coonskin caps

- ⊕ roller-skate keys
- ⊕ metal lunchboxes
- ⊕ S&H Green Stamps
- ⊕ 45-rpm records
- ⊕ slide rules
- ⊕ flashbulbs
- ⊕ home movie cameras
- ⊕ Dick and Jane readers

Kathryn and Allan Zullo

To stay young, hang out with your grandchildren. To get old in a hurry, try keeping up with them.

Grandma Jan

The Garden of Life

Get your lap ready. Something good is about to fall into it.

Judy Gattis Smith

The hearts of small children are delicate organs.

Carson McCullers

A grandmother was reading the Christmas story to her young granddaughter. The grandmother found it necessary to explain the phrase "Mary was great with child." When the little granddaughter finally understood the phrase, she clapped her hands excitedly and said, "Oh, goody, I hope it's a girl."

<u>The Observer</u>, October 1992

GRANDMOTHER TO GRANDSON WANDERING AROUND HER KITCHEN:

"What are you looking for?"

GRANDSON: "Nothing."

GRANDMOTHER: "You'll find it in that large jar where the cookies were."

Grandma Jan

There's one thing about children—they never go around showing snapshots of their grandparents.

Bob Phillips

Few things are more delightful than grandchildren fighting over your lap.

<u>The Lift Your Spirits Quote Book</u>

Take a deep, cleansing breath and don't push. That's probably one of the things your daughter or daughter-in-law is being told in preparation for childbirth. It's not bad advice for prospective grandparents as well!

Ruth Westheimer

There are no seven wonders of the world in the eyes of a child. There are seven million.

<u>The Lift Your Spirits Quote Book</u>

Isn't it crazy how our grandkids—

✪ can't drink a glass of milk without leaving a mustache above their upper lip.

✪ start with a gigantic wad of bubble gum in their mouth and it ends up in their hair.

✪ talk to their stuffed animals like they are people.

✪ eat most of the cookie dough before it goes into the oven.

✪ get toothpaste on everything but their teeth.

✪ put their sneakers on the wrong feet.

✪ study their belly buttons as if they were magical.

✪ try to hide two big stalks of broccoli under a thin potato skin.

✪ never seem to tire of fast-food.

✪ stick four fluorescent Band-Aids over one itsy-bitsy cut.

✪ can always bamboozle us into a toy store.

⊛ smush their faces against car windows, thinking they are amusing bypassing motorists.

⊛ insist on taking their security blanket everywhere.

Grandma Jan

Your children are your investment. Your grandchildren are your dividends.

Anonymous

If someone would tell me,
"Your grandchild has faults,"
I believe I would call
For my smelling salts.

Mary McBride

Every grandchild's birth changes us so fundamentally that we will always take a bit of their light with us as we live our lives.

Sue Johnson and Julie Carlson

A bonus of being a grandmother is being with babies and toddlers and rediscovering the delights of play.

Sheila Kitzinger

Becoming a grandmother is like having dessert. The best is saved for last.

Carolyn J. Booth and Mindy B. Henderson

Dear Granddaughter,
I love it when you—

- ❀ beg me to tell stories of my life over and over again.
- ❀ E-mail me with the message, "I love you, Grandma!"
- ❀ give me something special you created in school.
- ❀ snuggle up to me on the couch to watch TV.
- ❀ share your special secrets and dreams with me.
- ❀ hand me a flower picked from my garden.
- ❀ give me a big bear hug.
- ❀ surprise me with a weekend visit.
- ❀ treat me like your best friend.
- ❀ are asleep looking like an angel, so beautiful and peaceful.

Grandma Jan

Dear Grandson,

Nothing makes me so teary-eyed

as when I remember——

- ❀ the day you were born.
- ❀ you taking your first steps.
- ❀ you pointing at me and blurting out, "Gamma!"
- ❀ the night we put your first baby tooth under your pillow for the tooth fairy.
- ❀ how everyone was so happy when you were finally potty trained.
- ❀ the smile that jumps right into my heart, warming me up faster than a hot cup of chocolate.
- ❀ the look on your face when you got your first puppy.
- ❀ your eyes that sparkle with mischief and wonder.
- ❀ the special child who keeps me young at heart.

Grandma Jan

Spoil your grandchildren! . . . with the parent's permission, of course. It's a grandparent's right—and responsibility—as well as a grandchild's expectation.

Vicki Lansky

There is no time so short as the time between when the kids stop wrecking your furniture and your grandkids start.

Mary McBride

Top Ten Names for Grandmothers

1. Grandmother
2. Grandma
3. Granny
4. MawMaw
5. Nana
6. MiMi
7. Nannie
8. Me-Maw
9. Mama _____ (first or last name)
10. Grandmommy

Carolyn J. Booth and Mindy B. Henderson

We learn to be grandmothers, just as we learn to be mothers.

Sheila Kitzinger

First Grandchild

As if God saved the best for last,
With a gift from Heaven above;
Then sent it down on angel's wing,
In a tiny bundle of love.
The purest touch of Heaven,
God sent to live on earth;
Is there within your first grandchild,
In the miracle of its birth.
The first time that you hold them,
Nestled in your arms so sweet;
They somehow steal your heart away,
And make your life complete.
As if God saved the best for last,
They sent it from Heaven above;
This tiny babe on angel's wings,
Your first grandchild to love.

Allison Chambers Coxsey

Life is not always perfect, even for grandparents, but . . . the very best part comes when you feel two soft arms around your neck, and you hear the words, "I love you, Grandma!"

Lanie Carter

We can offer our grandchildren unconditional love, be a source of their roots, and be heard in ways that our own children can never hear us.

Vicki Lansky

If your baby is beautiful and perfect, never cries or fusses, sleeps on schedule, and burps on demand, an angel all the time . . . You're the grandma.

Teresa Bloomingdale

A teen's grandmother said she'd like to buy the adolescent some CDs and wondered how to choose them. The reply came quickly: "Easy, Gram . . . just listen to them, and if you can't stand the sound, I'll probably like 'em."

Eva Shaw

One of the reasons children are such duds socially is that they say things like "When do you think you're going to be dead, Grandma?"

Jean Kerr

GRANDMOTHER #1: "When your grandson graduates from college, what will he be?"

GRANDMOTHER #2: "At this rate, I figure at least 40!"

Grandma Jan

Children are the hands by which we take hold of heaven.

Henry Ward Beecher

The modern child will answer you back before you've said anything.

Laurence J. Peter

Your grandchild will not care if you live on a very restricted budget, believe me. Grandma is warm, cozy, and loving, and she always has time. To the child, that is what is important. Even if you do live near your grandchild—even if you make your home in some distant part of the country—you can be warm, close, and loving. You can set aside special times for sharing with your grandchild. And that is the greatest gift of all.

Lanie Carter

Ignorance is a painless evil; so, I should think, is dirt, considering the merry faces that go along with it.

George Eliot

How can one say no to a child? How can one be anything but a slave to one's own flesh and blood?

Henry Miller

A grandmother's heart bursts with pride when her grandchildren—

- ✿ always try their best.
- ✿ obey their parents.
- ✿ help others in need.
- ✿ are kind to animals.
- ✿ are good sports, win or lose.
- ✿ share their toys with friends.
- ✿ say something clever or funny.
- ✿ listen politely to what older people have to say.
- ✿ save part of their allowance in a piggy bank.
- ✿ are awarded gold stars for good citizenship.

Grandma Jan

Ending of a child's night prayer:

". . . and make me a good boy—oh,

never mind.

I don't have

to be good tomorrow.

We're going to Grandmom's."

Gene Perret

Children must invent their own games and teach
the old ones how to play.

Nikki Giovanni

Gifts and Treasures

Grandchildren love the way Grandma smells. I have been using the same type of perfume for years, and one time when the children were leaving, my eldest grandchild, who loved to sit on my lap, said, "I don't want to leave because I will miss the way Grandma smells."

On hearing that innocent plea, I quickly ran into the bedroom for a piece of cloth, stuffed cotton for a head, and tied a bow around the neck to make a doll. Then I sprayed the doll with my perfume, and gave it to my granddaughter.

She is fifteen years old now, and to this day every time she comes to visit, she brings the doll to get a couple of squirts of my perfume for it. Sometimes when I talk to her on the phone, she reminds me that it has been too long since our last visit because her doll has lost all of its smell.

The reminder of her love and how much she misses me is a subtle but powerful one.

Lanie Carter

Wherever children are, there is the golden age.

Novalis

Grandchildren amaze their grandmothers when they—

⊗ learn things so quickly.

⊗ act fearless when riding every scary ride at the amusement park.

⊗ shove half a bag of popcorn into their mouths.

⊗ have mastered playing video and arcade games.

⊗ are happy one moment, and throw a temper tantrum the next.

⊗ manage to read under the bed covers.

⊗ are so brave in the dentist's chair.

⊗ get up at the crack of dawn on Christmas morning.

⊗ are always one step ahead of adults.

Grandma Jan

Your grandchildren are the most beautiful leaves on the family tree.

Carolyn J. Booth and Mindy B. Henderson

"What did you bring me, Grandma?"
They ask when they are small.
They hope that you will answer,
"It's out in that big U-Haul."

Mary McBride

Definition of an Eight-Year-Old Grandson

A grandson is a combination of noise, energy, imagination, curiosity, and hunger. He is Grandma's spoiled little imp. A grandson is a growing animal of superlative promise to be fed, watered, and kept warm. If not washed too often, and if kept in a cool, quiet place after each accident, he will survive broken bones, swarms of bees, athletic encounters, fistfights, and six slices of pizza. A grandson is a periodic nuisance and a joy forever. The future is his, and he will inherit your world.

Grandma Jan

Definition of a Six-Year-Old Granddaughter

A granddaughter is a wee pixie with dirt on her face and stars in her eyes. Her joyful spirit and infectious smile are impossible to resist. A granddaughter is fun, creative, tender, and strong. She's a pain to little boys, but Grandma's little princess. In her you see the promise of a bright future, which you have the chance to help mold. When seen through a granddaughter's eyes, the universe greatly resembles paradise. It's such a sweet and delightful age; you hope that it's not just a passing stage.

Grandma Jan

Your grandma and your dog will always love you no matter what you do.

Matthew, age 10

A young couple dropped off their twin toddlers for Grandma to take care of while they took a much-needed vacation. They supplied her with all the baby paraphernalia, including an oversized playpen.

A few days later, the mother called Grandma to see how she was doing with her babysitting duties.

"Well, dear," she responded, "it's been touch and go, but thank you so much for the playpen. It is such a blessing. I spend a few hours every afternoon sitting in there with a glass of wine and a Danielle Steel novel. The twins are making a mess of the den, but they can't get near me."

Grandma Jan

Small wonder we love our grandchildren. They are our immortality.

Phyllis McGinley

Unless you are the victim, nothing is quite so funny as kids mimicking their elders.

Eva Shaw

Never show your grandchildren your class photo from high school. They may ask, "Which one is you?"

Gene Perret

Grandkids teach grandmothers—

- how to talk with imaginary playmates.
- there is no such thing as too tired.
- there is a Santa Claus, and a purple dinosaur.
- it's not easy housebreaking a puppy.
- to stop living in the Dark Ages and buy a computer.
- to laugh at themselves when they goof.
- what is cool and what is not.
- to stop driving like "little old ladies."
- to enjoy other music besides classical and the "golden oldies."
- to relax, put on jeans and a sweatshirt, and hang out.

Grandma Jan

When I Watch

When I watch my oldest son
With his little daughter,
Reading her books,
Or patiently braiding her hair,
Or waiting while she chooses, and changes her mind and
    chooses, and changes her mind about
What she will wear,
And when I watch him bathing her,
Or kissing a bump on her forehead to make it better,
Or tenderly tucking her into bed at night,
I know that, though I did a lot of things wrong,
I must have done a few things right.

Judith Viorst

Picture your grandchildren as a rose garden. Some will bloom beautifully. Others will need to be thorned to grow. Garden with the warmth of a smile, with patience and love. In your later years, your life will be a bed of roses.

Carolyn J. Booth and Mindy B. Henderson

Over the Rainbow

Grandmothers are wise and patient. They give others the benefit of the doubt and are quick to grant forgiveness and acceptance when blame and condemnation would seem a more natural response. Courage in hardship and grace in victory come naturally to them.

They know how to take the edge off criticism with a funny story and often make themselves the butt of jokes to defuse tension. They also know when to be serious, earning the respect of the generations with their insight, tenacity, and wisdom.

Arlene F. Benedict

A great-grandmother is a natural storyteller. She is a living family historian who remembers the fun and wonder of a gentler world.

Grandma Jan

My Nana is the only grown-up I know who always looks under her bed before she goes to sleep. My dad kids her about hoping to find the bogeyman.

Jenny, age 9

I never told Grandma how terrified I was because she was not like Mama, who always tried to soften the harshness of life for me. I knew Grandma believed in meeting reality head-on. She once told me, "Baby, life just ain't fair."

Claudia Limbert

I loved my grandmother more than any other human being because she never lied, never told you what you wanted to hear, never compromised. She had a healthy hatred for all living human beings, all systems of government, all religion, except her own, of course, which was based on her intolerance of humanity with a little Judaism thrown in.

Roseanne Barr

Grandmothers give their grandchildren confidence, teaching them to never fear shadows, for there is always a light shining somewhere nearby.

Grandma Jan

 As I was growing up, my grandmother taught me to do string tricks, and my grandfather made wonderful shadow pictures on the wall. In these days of TV and videos, these simple pleasures seem lost. Why not revive them for that special time with your grandchild?

Judy Gattis Smith

I guess it won't be too bad getting as old as Grandma. As long as I can have a younger boyfriend and jet around the world like she does.

Carrie, age 8

Grandma, When Were the Good Old Days?

Grandma, when were the good old days?
And why were they called that?
Do you wish that you were back there now
Instead of where you're at?

She made me stop and wonder.
I knew when I thought they were,
But why did we believe that?
I really wasn't sure!

You know, in now reflecting,
Is it really "the days" we miss?
Or the loss of FEARLESS innocence,
And untroubled childhood bliss?

Honey, my youth held good days,
But it held some bad ones too,

And I wouldn't trade ten-years-of-"then,"
For my loving days with you.

Yes, life was kinder, and simpler then,
But if I teach you very well,
You, too, will speak of "The Good Old Days"
And the stories Gram would tell.

Anna Mae Wittig

The grandchildren were always delighted to see her. . . .
They enjoyed her because she obviously enjoyed them.

Peregrine Churchill, grandson of Jeanie Jerome Churchill

It is safe to say that my grandmother never envisioned that she would have a granddaughter one day . . . and this granddaughter would have her own money, can shop—50 percent off, full price, doesn't matter, she never has to ask anyone's permission—because she makes her own living, doing what is important to her, which is to tell stories, many of them about her grandmother.

Amy Tan
"My Grandmother's Choice," <u>Ladies Home Journal,</u>
October 1996

Whatever happened to Grandma's brag book and the personal touch?

Too many grandmothers of the new millennium e-mail their children requesting a JPEG file of their new grandbabies to create a screen saver.

Grandma Jan

I thank God for my grandmother, who stood on the word of God and lived with the spirit of courage and grace.

Maya Angelou

A Grandmother's Wisdom

❀ Tell the truth no matter what the consequences, for honesty heals.

❀ Good manners and kindness can be more important than money or education.

❀ Being angry with people always hurts you more than it does them.

❀ Love what you do and always try to build a better world.

❀ Laugh at yourself and with yourself.

❀ Defeat is no disgrace, but apathy is.

❀ Unselfish love liberates everyone and everything.

❀ The best way of helping yourself is to make a good friend.

❀ Always believe in yourself and the beauty of your dreams.

❀ Your family will always be part of you; it isn't where you come from but where you're headed that counts.

❀ Never take life, friends, or family for granted.

Grandma Jan

Modern invention has banished the spinning wheel, and the same law of progress makes the woman of today a different woman from her grandmother.

Susan B. Anthony

Our mothers and grandmothers, some of them moving to music not yet written.

Alice Walker

The long look backward is also part of being a grandmother. In our concern for our grandchildren, we want them to learn "old-fashioned" morals and spiritual values such as honesty, courage, love, self-control, and reverence. Thus, we remember and share our stories. There were disappointments and adventures and ordinary things that brought us joy. These biographical anecdotes give color and reality to past generations.

Judy Gattis Smith

Only a grandmother can remember when we counted our blessings rather than our calories.

Grandma Jan

Grandparents should be one of a child's most valuable resources. They should be gentle teachers of the way life was, and the way it always should be.

John Rosemond

Ten-year-old Ronny announced to his grandma that he was sick of studying and was going out to play basketball. "Would you please do the rest of my homework for me?" he pleaded.

"I'm sorry," she responded. "It just wouldn't be right."

"Maybe not," he chuckled, "but why not give it a try anyway."

Anonymous

My grandmother used to say a day is wasted if you don't fall over at least once with laughter.

Luci Swindoll

If you plan to teach your grandchild the value of a dollar, you'd better not waste a moment!

Grandma Jan

Who knows more than Grandmother? Nobody! And if you don't believe it, just ask her.

Dr. Criswell Freeman

For me, Grandma's room itself was far more interesting than anything outside the window, because it held her many treasures.

Eudora Seyfer

A little boy and his grandmother were walking along the seashore when a huge wave appeared out of nowhere and swept the child out to sea. The grandmother, horrified, fell to her knees and said, "God, please return my beloved grandson. Please, I beg of you. Send him back safely." And, lo, another huge wave washed in and deposited the little boy on the sand at her feet. She picked him up, looked him over, and looking up at the sky, said, "He had a hat!"

A Pretty Good Joke Book

Discipline is the last thing that a father wants to consider because he doesn't like taking on tasks for which he has no talent. His only comfort is that no one else has any talent either. It is a game with seeded players. In fact, the great unspoken truth about child-raising is that, in spite of the 7,000 books of expert advice, the right way to discipline a child is still a mystery to most fathers, and to most mothers too. Only your grandmother and Genghis Khan knew how to do it.

Bill Cosby

Grandmothers are a vital source of wisdom and tradition, the stable center that holds while all around is in flux. Indeed, with the rapid changes in American society over the past decades, grandmothers have never been more important to us. They are providers of comfort and continuity. They teach us how to live and how to be happy—and sometimes, if we are good, they bake us cookies.

Armand Eisen

To Grams,

Just a minute honey
I cannot count the times
When this old familiar plea
My grandmother would chime

Just a minute honey
I pretend not to hear
I've got so many things to do
I try to make this clear

Just a minute honey
Would you bring me my purse
Reluctantly I turn around
Under my breath I curse

Just a minute honey
She reaches deep inside

The sea of treasured grandma things
And pulls out the bill with pride

You just let me know honey
If you need a little more
Ashamed of my impatience
I ask what is this for?

But I needn't hear the answer
I know it's just because
She loves me more than anything
That's all it ever was

Just a minute honey
As I'm walking out the door
I guess I could have listened
For just a minute more

Love, Jessica

At dinnertime, Grandma just winks when I reach under the table and feed my carrots to the dog.

Brian, age 5

A little boy asked his mother where he came from, and also where she had come from as a baby. His mother gave him a tall tale about a beautiful white-feathered bird. The boy ran into the next room and asked his grandmother the same question and received a variation on the bird story. He then scampered outside to his playmate with the comment, "You know, there hasn't been a normal birth in our family for three generations."

Howard Hendricks

One grandmother will spoil a baby. Two working together will bring him up in the way he should go, for each will suspect the other of spoiling him and will check it.

William Allen White

My grandmother taught me to believe in miracles.

Lilly Mary Vigil

I wish I would lose more teeth so I could cash in on Grandma's tooth fairy!

Jason, age 9

My grandmother was a very tough woman. She buried three husbands. Two of them were just napping.

Rita Rudner

Grandmothering is about praying and playing.

Anonymous

QUESTION: What is the favorite nine-letter word used by Jewish grandmothers?

ANSWER: Eateateat!

Isaac Asimov

If God intended us to follow recipes, he wouldn't have given us grandmothers.

Linda Henley

Life is a great mystery, except, of course, to grandmothers. Somehow, somewhere, grandmothers figured things out.

Dr. Criswell Freeman

The Grandmother Principles

1. The grandmother way is the easy way.
2. Grandmothers already have tenure.
3. Everything comes to an end eventually.
4. A grandmother is a safe haven.
5. There's nothing so simple that you cannot make it complicated if you really try.
6. The most powerful way to teach is by example.
7. People with *real* clout don't *have* to throw their weight around.
8. Grandmothers don't *have* to be politically correct.
9. When getting somebody else to do a task is more work than just doing it yourself, do it yourself.
10. Most arguments are about who is in charge.
11. It's always *safe* to talk to a grandmother.
12. Grandmothers *delegate*.

13. A grandmother is not a quarterback.

14. *Somebody* has to be the grown-up.

15. No sickness or injury is so bad that panic can't make it worse.

16. There are secret stories that only grandmothers should know.

17. It will be finished when it's finished.

18. Grandmothers plan for the long haul.

19. If it can't be done one way, it can be done another way.

20. After you give people something, it belongs to *them*.

21. For grandmothers, the light doesn't have to be perfect.

Suzette Haden Elgin

If a family has no grandparent, it has no jewel.

Chinese proverb

A grandmother can't be cloned! Each one is unique with her own distinctive personality. She possesses a magical wisdom that she instills in her grandchildren for the rest of their lives.

Grandma Jan

To forget one's ancestors is to be a brook without a source, a tree without a root.

Chinese proverb

Grandmothers, having raised the children who raise the children, possess special insights into family life. So when it comes to matters of house and home, wise kids and grandkids seek the advice of their clan's most experienced mother.

Dr. Criswell Freeman

I don't care what they say—Grandma really does have eyes in the back of her head!

Stacie, age 7

My grandmother was the one member of my immediate family who most understood me, or so I thought at the time. Looking back, I think it was not so much her understanding as it was the sheer force of her encouragement that helped me through those years.

Linda Sunshine

What Is a Grandmother?

She's younger than springtime
With stars in her eyes
Or a silver-haired angel
In a mortal's disguise.
When you're feeling let down
And a shadow appears,
Just the touch of her hand
Will banish your fears.

She's a practical nurse
Who knows how to heal;
And when a crisis arrives,
She is stronger than steel.

When a family has problems
As quick as you please

She straightens them out
With the greatest of ease.

She's adept at surprises
Or telling stories at night;
She's the cookie-jar keeper
And a grandchild's delight.
She knows all the angles
And what life is about—
A grandmother is someone
We couldn't do without.

Reginald Holmes

Everyone needs to have access both to parents and grandchildren in order to be a full human being.

Margaret Mead

Grandchildren will be full of admiration for a grandma who surfs the Net with them.

Selma Wasserman

A grandmother is a source of true inspiration to her grandchildren. When the rest of the world is too busy to slow down, she is willing to stop and listen. Her advice, when offered, is based on a world of experience. Her strength and love can have a profound and lasting effect on her grandchildren.

Mary Grace Rodarte

Showers of Love

When a grandmother looks at her grandchild, she sees perfection, because everything God creates is perfect.

Grandma Jan

I couldn't believe it when my grandmother had a heart with my name tattooed on her ankle. You can't see it very well under her support hose, but it's kinda embarrassing!

Tammy, age 13

Grandmothers understand the power of love, and they share that message with the entire family. A grandmother shares her love through words and more importantly—through deeds. The beneficiaries of that love are forever blessed.

Mary Carlisle Beasley

What do your grandchildren call you? I would suspect that whatever it is, you were thrilled with it. I'm sure something special happened when you became Mimi, Nana, G-Mom or Mamaw. Maybe it was something you said or did, or maybe it was just the name that past generations in your family have used. In any case, you all have your own story. You are that special person who will always answer when they call, always listen when they speak, and always love them no matter what they do. You are their grandmother.

Chrys Howard

My grandmother made me feel as if I were the only baby, girl, and woman capable of stealing her heart so completely. In her eyes I was truly grand—one of a kind, cherished as though I were the only grandchild ever born on this earth. And that was her gift to me.

Traci Mullins

We should all have one person who knows how to bless us despite the evidence. Grandmother was that person to me.

Phyllis Therox

Let your grandchildren know, through words and deeds, that the bond of affection that attaches the two of you to one another can never be broken.

Arthur Kornhabler

The sense of euphoria—pure and heightened with each birth of a grandchild—is some kind of magic. To rethink the moment I held that first, tiny bundle, or to imagine the face of the ninth whom I've yet to see, causes me to be heady, and my heart quickens—yet again!

Grandma Romaine

The Grandparent Credo

1. Grandparents give time.

2. Grandparents give love.

3. Grandparents give gifts.

4. Grandparents think big.

5. Grandparents are good sports.

6. Grandparents are patient and understanding.

7. Grandparents are always supportive and enthusiastic.

8. Grandparents don't disagree with parents in front of the grandchildren.

9. Grandparents are devoted to their grandchildren.

10. Grandparents are fun.

11. Grandparents are indispensable.

Susan Newman

The strength of my conscience came from Grandma, who meant what she said. Perhaps nothing is more valuable for a child than an adult who is firm and loving—and Grandma was loving.

Margaret Mead

Kind words can be short and easy to speak, but their echoes are truly endless.

Mother Teresa

To love is to receive a glimpse of heaven.

Karen Sunde

Grandparents are more patient, more tolerant, more aware of little changes in their grandchild.

Nancy Reagan

So Many Grandmas!

Millions of grannies, all in a row
Which one is mine? How will I know?

Ma-maw, Mi-ma, Nona, Oma,
Grandy, Grammers, Grandma, Gran

Tall ones, skinny ones, chubby ones too,
All colors and sizes, old ones and new.

There's Mimi, Mahna, Gram, Granny,
Gramma, Namma, Mamma Sal, and Nanny.

A buffet of grandmas, each one a delight.
But how will I know? Which one is right?

Oh! There she is—see, over there?
I'd know her for sure, anytime, anywhere!

How did I know? It's easy, you see—
She's the one with all the pictures of ME!!

Karen Hill

Compared to my mother and her friends, with their bobbed hair, knee-length dresses from Marshall Field's and high-heeled pumps, Grandma looked odd and old-fashioned—like a picture book of Mother Goose rhymes. . . . We loved each other with an unspoken devotion: I was her only grandchild and she was my only living grandparent.

Eudora Seyfer

What can you do to promote peace? Go home and love your family.

Mother Teresa

Here's my advice: Make sure your children and grandchildren know you love them.

Barbara Bush

Love does not dominate; it cultivates.

Goethe

I want future generations to remember my good advice, but most of all I want them to remember my love.

Heather Whitestone

Becoming a grandmother brings the satisfaction of giving and receiving love, sometimes more freely and more generously than ever before.

Sheila Kitzinger

Grandmothers never forget—

- ❀ a grandchild's birthday.
- ❀ a major holiday.
- ❀ their grandchild's school plays, music recitals, or sports events.
- ❀ special family gatherings.
- ❀ nicknames of grandchild's close friends and pets.
- ❀ what kinds of things kids like to do.
- ❀ their families' favorite vacation spots.
- ❀ the best hamburger and pizza places in town.
- ❀ their grandchild's hopes and dreams.

Grandma Jan

All grandparents, cool and otherwise, are complete pushovers and will do practically anything to hear those magic words: "I love you, Grandma," "I love you, Grandpa."

Leslie Linsley

I dig being a mother . . . and, of course, as a grandmother, I just run amok.

Whoopi Goldberg

Grandmothers want to be remembered by their grandchildren as—

- ❀ their favorite babysitter.
- ❀ the world's best storyteller.
- ❀ someone who was always there for them!
- ❀ a lifelong friend and playmate.
- ❀ a trusted keeper of all of their secrets.
- ❀ their biggest fan.
- ❀ a special loved one who made a difference in their lives.
- ❀ someone who accepted them just the way they were.
- ❀ a good person who always tried to stand up for what was right and true.
- ❀ their beloved grandmother.

Grandma Jan

Most grandmothers touch a lot. They hug, they stroke, they pat, and they cuddle. Even after we're grown, they find ways to run their hand over our backs or ruffle our hair. Somehow, although they may have as many irons in the fire as parents do, they find more time to make physical contact with their grandchildren; and the grandchildren never forget.

Kristen Johnson Ingram

The best and most beautiful things in the world cannot be seen or even touched. They must be felt with the heart.

Helen Keller

A Grandmother's Heart

On Mother's Day my thoughts go back
      to all the years that have gone before,
And all my love and good wishes
      go straight to that open door.
For always the door to your heart and home
      stood open with welcoming cheer
And memories of you, Grandmother
      grow dear with each year.

Helen Steiner Rice

Many years from now when your grandchildren are grown and have children of their own, they will reminisce and tell stories about you, unlocking a tiny time of love energy flooding their souls with sweet memories.

Be very clear, don't stop growing, stay in the flow of life.

Judy Ford

My grandma rates right up there with Barbie and Santa Claus.

Tiffany, age 7

My grandma is loving and kind—that is until somebody tries to mess with me.

Timothy, age 10

Where there is lasting love, there is a family.

Shere Hite

Toss aside your embarrassment about how you look playing in the sandbox or giving your special bear hug at the nursery school door and revel in knowing that your grandchild only has eyes for the wonderful person you are inside. That's the magic of the love between grandchild and grandparent.

Sue Johnson and Julie Carlson

The Season
of Wisdom

More Perks of Grandmotherhood

✾ You stop sweating the small stuff.

✾ Your sense of purpose flourishes.

✾ You take more chances, even if you look foolish.

✾ The quality of your life is measured by every small kindness.

✾ You rekindle a lifetime philosophy in which the concept of love is once again your focus.

✾ You make more time for friends.

✾ You live at your own pace.

✾ You accept more, and criticize less.

✾ You look forward to new challenges.

✾ You become a better listener.

✾ You start taking interest in the activities of youth.

✾ You no longer long for the "good old days," looking forward to each new day.

✾ You thank a higher power for all your blessings.

Grandma Jan

National Grandparents Day

The impetus for a National Grandparents Day originated with Marian McQuade, a housewife in Fayette County, West Virginia. Her primary motivation was to champion the cause of lonely elderly in nursing homes. She also hoped to persuade grandchildren to tap the wisdom and heritage their grandparents could provide. President Jimmy Carter, in 1978, proclaimed that National Grandparents Day would be celebrated every year on the first Sunday after Labor Day.

National Grandparents Day Web Site

If grandparents want to have a meaningful and constructive role, they must learn that becoming a grandparent is not having a second chance at parenthood.

Eda LeShan

My eyes misted at the sign of my granddaughter handling her own child. Not too long ago, I had stood this way and watched my daughter doing the same things with Dena (my granddaughter).

Betty Baum

My mother was delighted when she became a great-grandmother, that is until she suddenly realized she was the mother of a grandfather.

Grandma Jan

Every year when Great-Grandma has a birthday cake, we keep the fire extinguisher handy.

Laurie, age 8

GRANDDAUGHTER: "Grandma, really! I'm absolutely shocked that at your age you bought yourself a see-through negligee."

GRANDMOTHER: "Relax, dear. At this age, your grandfather can't see through anyway."

<u>3650 Jokes, Puns, and Riddles</u>

Almost all grandmothers agree that grandparenting is easier than parenting.

Judith Stevens-Long

Even now I am not old. I never think of it, and yet I am a grandmother to eleven children. I have seventeen great-grandchildren.

Grandma Moses

My great-grandma walks kind of slow. It's either because her joints need lubricating or she doesn't work or go to school so she thinks she has all the time in the world.

Tanya, age 7

By the time you reach great-grandmotherhood, your entire wardrobe consists of polyester clothes with elastic waistbands.

Mary Mackie

Tradition is the practice of handing down stories, beliefs, and customs from one generation to another in order to establish and reinforce a strong sense of identity.

J. Otis Ledbetter and Tim Smith

Enjoy your position as matriarch. It is a great achievement to have three generations of descendants.

Eleanor Berman

This is just a small sampling of exceptional Grand Dames who didn't let age keep them from being super achievers.

At the age of . . .

- *70*—Golda Meir was elected Prime Minister of Israel.
- *77*—Louise Nevelson designed the interior of the Chapel of the Good Shepherd in St. Peter's Church, New York.
- *79*—Emily Greene Baleh, co-founder of the Women's International League for Peace and Freedom, won the Nobel Prize.
- *82*—Thelma Pitt-Turner completed the Hastings (New Zealand) Marathon in 7 hours, 58 minutes.
- *87*—Mary Baker Eddy founded *The Christian Science Monitor*.
- *91*—Maude Tull of California got her first driver's license.
- *95*—Martha Graham premiered her latest choreographed work, *Maple Leaf Gala*.

❁ *100*—Gwen Ffangcon-Davies, legendary British stage actress for eight decades, appeared in the movie *The Master Blackmailer*, and was also made a Dame by the Order of the British Empire.

Andrew Postman

Time and trouble will tame an advanced young woman, but an advanced old woman is uncontrollable by any earthly force.

Dorothy L. Sayers

I have the best of three worlds. I got to stay at my great-grandma's ranch with all the horses, my grandma's condo right across from Disneyland, and then come home to my house with a swing set and a pool.

Annie, age 8

Inside every seventy-year-old is a thirty-five-year-old asking: "What happened?"

Ann Landers

With age a grandmother grows wiser. She talks less, and says more.

Grandma Jan

Youth is a gift of nature; age is a work of art.

Anonymous

When grace is joined with wrinkles, it is adorable. There is an unspeakable dawn in a happy old age.

Victor Hugo

I could not, at any age, be content to take my place by the fireside and simply look on. Life was meant to be lived. Curiosity must be kept alive. One must never, for whatever reason, turn his back on life.

Eleanor Roosevelt

The Swanson women are four generations of entrepreneurs. My great-grandma is Chairman of the Board, my grand-mother is President, my mother is Head Accountant, and I work part-time in the sales office after school.

Michelle, age 16

Every time I think I'm getting old, something else happens.

Lillian Carter

When you cease to contribute, you begin to die.

Eleanor Roosevelt

A great-grandma is an older lady who never says, "Hurry up!" or "I don't have time."

Aaron, age 10

Many great-grandparents today are living active lives. Through their great-grandchildren their lives are extended even further into the future they will never see.

Dr. Lillian Carson

Great-Grammy was a "Rosie the Riveter" in World War II. I don't know exactly what that was, but it sounds like something out of *Star Wars*.

Aaron, age 10

Surely the consolation prize of old age is finding out how few things are worth worrying over.

Dorothy Dix

A family's history is like a novel in progress with a full cast of characters and, because each of this is a part of you, you want to know them all.

Frederick Waterman

I wish I could become a time traveler and go back to see my great-grandma as a kid.

Blossom, age 12

We inherit from our ancestors gifts so often taken for granted. . . . We are links between the ages, containing past and present expectations, sacred memories, and future promise. Only when we recognize that we are heirs can we truly be pioneers.

Edward C. Sellner

Great-grandmothers are living icons. What wonderful stories they can share about a world before television, space travel, computers, and Madonna.

Grandma Jan

Life is what we make it
Always has been
Always will be.

Grandma Moses

I've decided to stop fussing about getting older. After all, if I stop getting older, I'm dead.

Great-Gramma Faye

And finally, take good care of yourself. Somebody's going to live to be a hundred, and it might as well be you.

Marie T. Freeman

Grandma Jan Says

As a grandmother I'm a perpetual student who never stops learning. How lucky I am to have the best teachers in the world—my four grandchildren—Cory, Bri, Chase and Dylan.

Bettye "MiMi" Flynn

Isn't it true that a grandmother, with a little help from a guardian angel, can fix anything?

Grandma Jan

Grandmothers plant the seeds of love into a child's heart—and they bloom forever.

Grandma Jan

A grandmother may become discouraged, but when it comes to her grandchildren, she is a cockeyed optimist.

Grandma Jan

Time goes by too fast! It seems that no sooner have we retired the rocking horse to the attic, than it has to be gotten down again.

Grandma Jan

You thought you were radiant when you were pregnant, but it's nothing like the glow of becoming a grandmother.

Grandma Jan

Grandmothers of the twenty-first century are a new breed of matriarchs who carry on in style. They're attractive, positive, energetic, and live every day to its fullest.

Grandma Jan

Take heart. A gift or talent your grandchild inherits from you will eventually surface.

Grandma Jan

Grandmothers have that knack of treating each grandchild like he or she is the most important person in the universe.

Grandma Jan

I could afford all the things I dreamed about as a kid if I didn't have grandchildren. But it is worth it!

Grandma Jan

To a grandmother, forgiveness is just another gift of love.

Grandma Jan

Can you think of a more magical place than Grandma's kitchen?

Grandma Jan

It's uncanny how a grandmother can see the light at the end of almost any tunnel.

Grandma Jan

A grandmother who is in touch with her inner child is tuned in to the joys and sorrows of the stages of youth.

Grandma Jan

There is a bond between grandmothers and grandchildren that can never be erased or broken, no matter what the circumstances and distances that part them.

Grandma Jan

We are still a generation of cookie-baking grandmas. Almost every jet-set grandma is in possession of an awesome family chocolate chip recipe that rivals Mrs. Fields's secret ingredients.

Grandma Jan

It's true that you can't buy your grandchildren's love. But can you think of a better reason for them to keep in touch?

Grandma Jan

Only a grandmother's love can stop time. She cares when nobody else cares, and keeps the faith when everyone else has given up.

Grandma Jan

Naomi Judd and Loretta Lynn might be the rare grandmothers who were honored with awards by The Recording Academy, but don't most grandmas deserve a Grammy®?

Grandma Jan

Be careful; you never know when your grandchild may catch a dream from you.

Grandma Jan

Expand your circle of love. There are so many children out there without grandparents, who are looking for words of encouragement and a hug.

Grandma Jan

Even a Picasso can't compare in value with all the family photos covering Grandma's wall.

Grandma Jan

Keep company with children. Their love of life is contagious.

Grandma Jan

Even the grandmother who is forced to face reality accepts it with love and understanding.

Grandma Jan

The more often you feel your own happiness, the more your grandchildren will be drawn to you.

Grandma Jan

Grandmothers may not have all the answers to their grandchildren's problems. . . . Then again, perhaps they do.

Grandma Jan

Permissions

ABOUT THE AUTHOR

Janet Lanese is the author of seven books celebrating special family members. Lanese was also a real estate broker, a writer for her local newspaper, a co-hostess for a local television program, and a contributing editor for over thirty magazines. During her life, Lanese enjoyed her roles as community volunteer and grandmother to three. She was a resident of Castro Valley, California.